COMPENDIUM
BITS AND PIECES
By Tonya Holmes Shook

Tonya Holmes Shook began her saga with art long before she ever went to school. As a little child her mother would teach her words by going through a catalog pointing to pictures. She learned image information and appreciation in this manner aiding a natural born curiosity which more than likely influenced artistic directions.

Pencil drawing was the first medium as a wee child which progressed to pastels and water colors then to her first oil painting by age ten. At age eleven and twelve Tonya experienced deadlines for the Tucumcari, New Mexico newspaper doing political cartoons after winning first in the Quay County Fair.

After a year of newspaper submissions an interval of several years transpired, interests changed at fourteen with her first art lessons in oil. Octogenarian, Mrs. Zula Mae Prunty, taught her from small prints of the masters and how to mix colors in oil. Animals and portrait work were her favorite topics.

No more art lessons were had until Tonya took summer school classes at U.N.M. after graduating high school. A boyfriend took some of her work to the professor's home for him to see so she could get admitted to his sophomore class. She was admitted, finishing up with an A for her work in his class. Carolene and Lance Folse of Denton,Texas own an acrylic painting where her adventure to depict texture first seriously began in 1954.

Very little training followed. Only after joining Snyder's Palette Club did she see programs where demonstrations from other artists occurred. She gives God credit to being her art teacher. Many times when difficult situations arrived during painting sessions it was after petitions in prayer when He dug her out from the blockade. Tonya says, "What you see is God taught."

Tonya Holmes Shook's art has soloed in many places over the years. An artsy eatery in Oklahoma City called "Flips" hosted her art for a session, the Brownstone Gallery in Huston hosted her and others listed in The Best of Texas catalog as well as being shown in Ft. Worth, Old Central on the Oklahoma State University campus, Union Bank in Austin, and The Cherokee Strip Museum in Perry, Oklahoma, to name a few. Eastern New Mexico University did a fourteen documentary of her art in the early 1980's hosted by Don Criss on a show titled "Things You Should Know." For a month Tonya had a piece titled, "Afternoon Tea", hang in Austin at the State Capital. It was painted from a Mart, Texas photo,. She has won numerous awards over the years in many annual type shows. Tonya has taught art to adults and children at art galleries she and her husband, Clarence, owned in Wichita Falls and at the ghost town business operated in Hastings, Oklahoma.

Her paintings consist of a number of bodies of works from different themes. As she was developing her thoughts about her lost heritage, she used the sepia-tone oils - a limited palette. One color, raw umber, is used with different shading from white to accomplish her historic pieces. Overlapping this theme, a mixture of full palette mixed with limited palette was done to combine the past and present. With a full palette philosophical themes were depicted with pearls among other common elements. Then lastly, a long and abiding interest in flowers is done in full palette. The most recent medium she is working with has been colored pencils. This medium is challenging to depict textures and is creating a new understanding never explored before. By using a wax base, she has learned how to blend some drawings with turpentine to mimic watercolor.

The Lord my Teacher was,
To do this piece of art,
Any pleasure received,
Give credit to Him,
For this would warm my heart.

Compendium
2014 copyright by Tonya Holmes Shook

Shook, Tonya Holmes   1935

ISBN 13 978-1500916190
ISBN 10 1500916196

Table of Contents

BITS AND PIECES

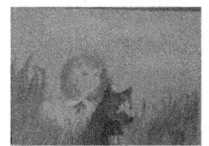 NFS

Pals: panel # 1

At age ten Tonya painted this piece for her friend in Oklahoma she was so homesick to see since she and her family moved to New Mexico. Her pal, Edilynn Turner (now Card) of Chickasha, Oklahoma, gave it back to her to show in other shows for a point of reference from then to now. Everyone starts somewhere. It was her first oil painted sixty-nine years ago.

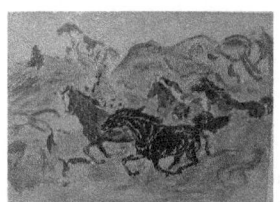 NFS (framed 24hx29w)

Stampeding Horses: (water color) panel # 1

First competition at age eleven. Won Blue Ribbon for all age category at Quay Co. Fair, Tucumcari, NM. Fall of 1946.

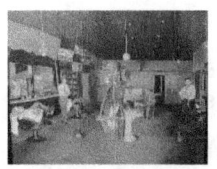 price: $995.00 (framed 30hx36w)

Porter King's Barber Shop: panel #1

(Photo courtesy of Scurry County Museum)

Porter King's Barber Shop, also known as "The Sanitary

Barber Shop," operated in Snyder in the early 1900's. Porter King is standing beside the barber's chair on the right side. The man in the front barber's chair is the father of C. L. Nobles. Mr. King had eight bathtubs in the rear room for the use of cowboys and they were supplied by water tanks on the top of his building. He sent his client's laundry to Fort Worth via the R.S. & P. through Roscoe and then on the T. & P. railroads. (The artist and her husband's home - written up in the Coffee-Table Book by Charles Garrett, *Stone-Tree Houses Of Texas*, was originally built by Porter King in the late 1800's) *Courtesy of the Scurry County Museum.*

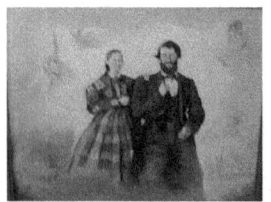 price: $595.00   (framed 25hx28w)

Elias & Regina Dowell: panel #1

This is of the artist's great grandparents who came from Carthage, Missouri to stake their land in the Cherokee Strip, west of Perry. Paintings related to this couple are ghosted in the background. Regina was born on the ship coming to America from Germany. Her sister was Elias' first wife and died leaving him with two daughters and a son without a mother. She married her brother-in-law and they had two children, Lena and the artist's grandfather, Elmer Fredrick Dowell. Elias died of pneumoni from getting caught in a "blue norther" when he went for supplies at Mulhall. Regina held on and cultivated their farm with help from some neighbors, the Keatings, only to die shortly after meeting obligations for the farm became theirs. Elmer was orphaned at ten. The farm has many stories it could tell. It still remains in the Dowell lineage.

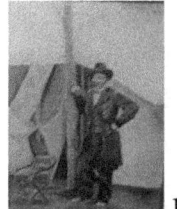 price: $995.00 (framed 32hx26w)

Ulysses S. Grant: panel #1

The first sepia-tone oil ever painted began with this Mathew Brady piece. Tonya was in the midst of research for their lost family heritage and the first visual stepping stones were paintings of the Civil War. She painted Lee next with bullet holes piercing the background and filled with depictions of war captured by Mathew Brady's camera. Sadly this piece has been destroyed during a temper fit of an individual looking for something to vent his rage on.

A number of people have owned Grant beginning with the artist's son who gave it to his father to hang in his law office. When the father died it came back to the artist's son. He was tragically killed in a motor cycle accident and it then reverted back to the artist.

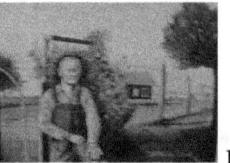 price: $50.00 (framed 16hx18w)

Elmer Fredrick Dowell: panel #1

Many little things of significance to the artist were recorded in this little folksy piece. The depiction is on the north side of an Oklaholma homestead. In the background to the right one can see a chicken house covered with roofing tar paper. There was another unseen one just like it far to the left of this piece, lined in a row. When both doors were opened in the houses a perfect alignment formed for the artist's cousin to sprint through while a mean rooster chased her once. You can see a tree on the far left, which was at the end of a row of trees, another three rows just like the first row was behind it to the north of the house forming a wind brake. Summer playtime under the shade was enjoyed by the artist, her sister and two cousins. A make-shift trellis behind Elmer bore tiny pink roses, Rose's handiwork. (Elmer's wife.) And last but not least, you see a bit of a large cedar tree on the far right. This is significant for what these little farm people instilled in all it's inhabitants and decendents. This frugal couple lived and taught by example. Rose cut the top of the cedar tree out to make the Christmas tree where all her family congregated to sing Christmas carols and exchange simple, mostly handmade, gifts once a year.

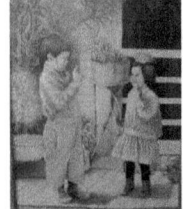 price: $250.00 (framed 32hx25w)

Uh Oh!: panel #1

Taken from an actual black and white photo, it was transformed into a folksy art form in color. Little sister attempted to work in flower pots like mother but had a mishap. Little brother censures his sibling but unknown to both of them is the shadowy figure of their mother behiind the screen door. Parts of history is recorded visually, this folksy rendition with objects of the past i.e. a screen door, clothing and even quaint architecture.

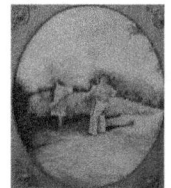 price: $450.00 (framed 24hx19w)

Saying Goodbye: panel #1

The artist's grandmother, grandfather and uncle saying "goodbye" to her grandfather's sister, Nora Roberts, and her husband Bob. Nora was one of two sets of twins in her grandfather's family. This sandy old farm was the artist's family destination from Jackboro, Texas when they came up the Chisholm Trail in a covered wagon in 1916. The hump in the background was a cellar storing all the canned goods and providing shelter during storms that frequented this part of the country. Kerosene lamps and a cot was a staple for this cellar. The water well is behind and from it came fresh water pumped into the house made possible by the artist's father. Many happy times were lived here, many farewells said much like what has been portrayed.

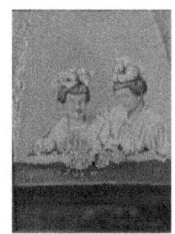 price: $40.00   (framed 12hx10w)

Sisters: panel #1

Always interested in life of the common man, clothing and hair styles are points of interest. Flowers played a large part in everyday life especially during the summertime. Often nosegays were put in the hair for portaits to be made.

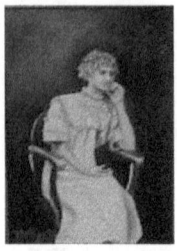 price: $35.00 (framed 12hx10w)
Pondering: panel #1

Folksy art depicting clothing during the early 1900's and stylized portraiture. Found photo from an early day album.

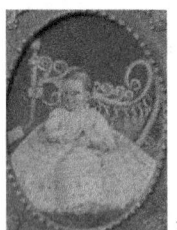 price: $40.00 (framed 10hx7w)
**Baby Bertha:** panel #1

A folksy art piece is done of the artist's Aunt Bertha whose clothing is handmade by Tonya's grandmother, Beulah Holmes, who was an expert tatter. This chair is jute woven.

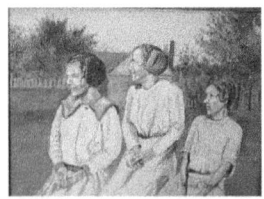 price: $30.00
**Three Aunts:** panel #1   (framed 9hx11w)

Salt of the earth women, hard workers and full of conversation, so much so no one listened only talked when they got together! The artist was privileged to have met one, Aunt Lonie, who lived in Tucumcari but never met her until she married her husband, Clarence.

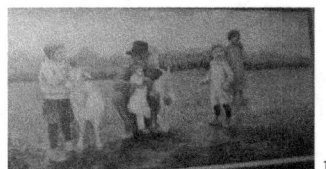 price: $800.00 (framed 32hx57w)

Old Goats, Children & a Little Bit of Time: panel #2

Grandpa Clark, living somewhere around Eastland County, TX with a number of children evoked the title as a pun on words from a once upon a time popular song. He was a friend of the artist's mother-in-law in an area where she grew up. The idea in a little bit of time even the little children, if they were lucky, would grow up to take the place of the elderly Mr. Clark.

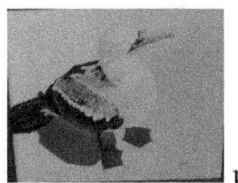 price: $195.00 (framed 27hx31w)

Web Feet: panel #2

One of God's creatures created among millions wears a beautiflul coat with intriguing designs. Even the simplest of forms can perk human interests.

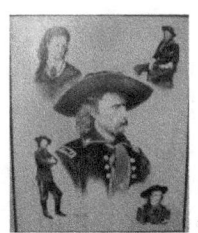 price: $895.00 (framed 37hx30w)

Through It All: panel #2

Another early day sepia-tone art piece used as a stepping stone in researching for a lost family heritage, _Disiplaced Cherokee: Come Home,Come home_ (a First Award

Winner in an Open Class Category at the 1986 Oklahoma State Fair.) This painting has many of Custer's images but the topic of interest is his wife, Elizabeth Custer. It was her loyalty and love for her husband through all the speculations and talk denouncing this General's battle tactics against the Native Americans that drew Tonya's attention to painting it. She never gave up defending his honor until the day she died.

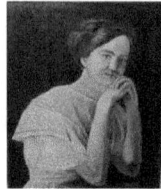 price: $100.00 (framed 28hx23)

Wedding Day: panel #2

Wedding day for a lady who lived on York Street in Wichita Falls, Texas. Done in a folksy fashion verses realism lends to the aura of "once upon a time."

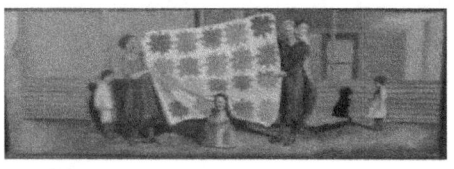 price: $125.00 (framed 8hx21w)

Quilting: panel #2

Beside quilting at the school house on the week end or evenings, communities came together in homes where a quilting rack was hoisted up onto the ceiling when not in use. The artist's grandmother is on the left in this very folksy depiction and her grandfather's sister, Aunt Lena is on the right side. All sorts of entertainment could be had by doing important chores. Quilting was one of them. Quilts have been treasured for generations when that used to be a necessity not a luxury. Tonya's generation came in on the tail end of this exercise, bits and pieces of the past.

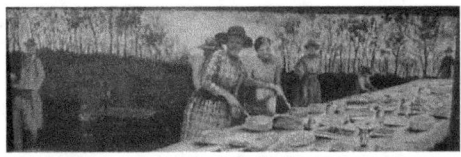 price: $125.00 (framed 8hx21w)

Dinner on the Grounds: panel # 2

Whether the occasion was a meal after church or for any other reason the lack of air-conditioning made this outdoor meal something to look forward to. Parents had time to talk and visit while the kids found friends to play with. Sometimes a game of horsehoes was played or maybe a try at croquet was the challenge, it was genuine relaxation. Chores took up most of the week's activity whether you were an adult or a kid but these long tables burdened with scrumptious home cooked food were cause for memories of such to linger over the years.

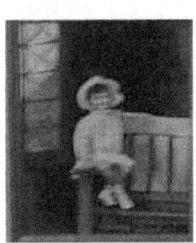 price: $35.00 (framed 10hx9w)

Sunday Best: panel #2

Another recording in that folksy way preserving the concept of dressing up in our finest for church day. This piece was actually taken from a personal album. Another bits and pieces of how American used to do things.

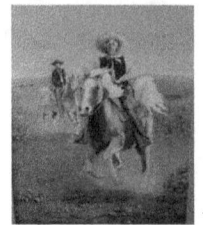 price: $160.00 (framed 26hx22w)

80 John Wallace & Mr. Mann: panel #2

The artist's own rendition of 80 John Wallace, a black man born into slavery in 1860 to becoming a millionaire from Mitchell County fame. 80 John lived in Lorain. He has public institutions named after him in Colorado City. 80 John was an uncommon man with integrity and smarts to grow his wages from riding drag in a cattle drive to that of millionaire. Clay Mann, his former boss and friend took 80 John under his wing and gave him advice, which he took, to becoming a man held with high esteem throughout Texas. He was a member of Texas and Southwestern Cattle Raisers Assoc. for over thirty years.

The face is actually from a photograph of him as an old man, the only one available. Courtesy of the steed he is riding (named Halo, an award winner), goes to Halo's owner, Megan Land Fowler of Krum, Texas, who is quite a little cowgirl herself. She graciously loaned a photo of her riding this moving dynamo for to me to use in this painting.

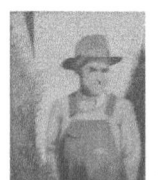 price: $695.00 (framed 21hx18w)

Grandpa: panel #3

Claud Washington Holmes, 1883-1950, taught the artist how to squirrel hunt, burst watermelons open and eat them on the way to the creek to hunt and how to wash the sticky off in the cold running stream of water as they took a sip. Memories of the common man, poor as can be yet rich in spirit, stuck to the artist and gave a sense of direction in her lifetime, art-journey sixty-nine years ago. Bits and pieces of life have been depicted in numerous ways and largely were influenced by this dear, sweet man. The year insulin for diabetes was discovered was when "Wash" learned he had that dreaded disease, a death warrant until that discovery.

price: $550.00 (framed 20hx24w)
George Marion Elkins Ranch: Kent County, panel #3

The photo was taken circa 1882 and was the ranch headquarters of George Marion Elkins who established his ranch on Mackenzie Creek near Mackenzie Mountains in 1877 or 1878. I assume the house was built around that time. The ranch was sold in 1911 to W. E. Connell and George opened a feed store in Post the same year. (Source: Kin Elkins, Abilene, TX) *(courtesy of Norman Wayne Brown, author and friend of the artist)*

price: $1,200.00 (framed 35hx29w)
"Black Moon", Leonard Riddles : panel #3

Being close friends, Leonard's wife, Eva, asked Tonya to paint her husband's portrait for the lobby of the Anadarko, OK Indian Museum to introduce his art show there. After painting it, the piece was not allowed because she has no

Indian card though is of Cherokee and German decent. The black moon with a "squiggly" at the top is the way the Comanche's name is depicted on a piece of art. All the visions piercing the night sky surrounding Black Moon are images of stories he learned from the old sages living on farms around Walters, OK. He would get off his tractor at noon and walk to their homes then drew pictures on his lunch sack of the stories they talked about. Later he transferred them to his canvas or animal skin. Leonard was asked with some other Indians to identify names of Indians in photographs at the Smithsonian. (Leonard is related to the artist way back through the Riddle line. His father was Cherokee. Both are now deceased.)

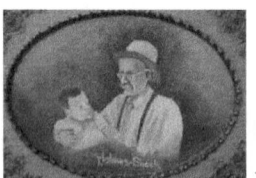 price: $795.00 (framed 28hx24w)

Once Upon a Time: panel: #3

C. E. Holmes as a baby. His dad was one of 3 men playing sandlot baseball in Jacksboro, Texas who were asked to come to Rice University to play ball. Two of them, C. E.'s dad and his brother, refused to go but the other one went. His name was Roger Hornsby. C.E. used to wear his dad's baseball uniform to play dress up in until he wore it out.

price: $35.00 (framed 7hx9w)

Fifth Generation: panel #3

A very primitive rendition folksy piece of the artist's

son, Randall Maxwell, and the artist's great grandfather, Robert Hatton King of Bowie, Texas.

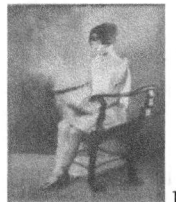 price: $800.00 (framed 27hx23w)

The Young Dutchess: panel #3

The dress she wore was hand made by her mother and perfectly tailored in every detail. This little farm girl had the air of a princess though a hard worker. Coming from a Dutch/Irish and German heritage, Dorothy reached beyond her station in life and actually became known as the Duchess where her husband worked, Texas Refinery Corp. They attended conventions held all over the world beside Fort Worth. The play on words was because of her background. The portrait is of the artist's mother.

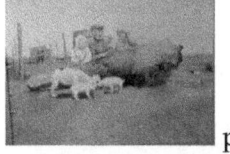 price: $650.00 (framed 32hx38w)

The Murphree Kids of Scurry County: panel#3

A local resident had given this photo to the museum and it attracted the author's attenion when the museum allowed her to select some pieces to paint from. After choosing it she learned it was from one of her dearest friends and a fellow Sunday School associate, Dorothy Murphree (Rosson), the bonneted baby.

(photo courtesy of Scurry County Museum)

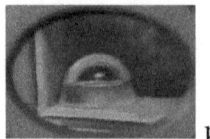 price: $30.00 (framed 7hx9w)

Grandma's Iron: panel #3

Tonya's grandmother once used an iron like this that was heated on her wood burning kitchen stove. In fact, at a young age she even ironed a little with this heavy iron. White starched shirts could get scorched easily if one didn't watch out!

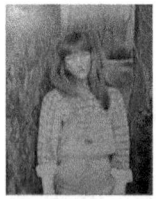 price: $450.00 (framed 35hx29w)

Some Days Are Diamonds... : panel #4

Mixing the full palette with a limited one gave a challenge to a painting of Tonya's daughter, Shanna. All the background was done in sepia-tone oil with the actual portrait in a full palette. _Some Days_, as the title just simply implies, were stones too and this was one of them

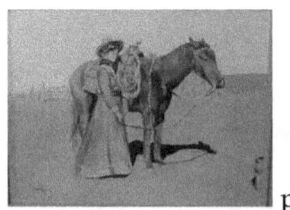 price: $450.00 (framed 18hx21w)

Fannie Hardin Fox: panel #4

Fannie was the wife of C. O. Fox and was a cousin of the infamous John Wesley Hardin written about in the recent book by Chuck Parsons and Norman Wayne Brown (Tonya's author friend): *A Lawless Breed: John Wesley Hardin, Texas Reconstruction, and Violence in the Wild West.* (photo courtesy of Scurry County Museum)

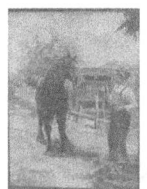 price: $450.00 (framed 21hx18w)
Ole Doc: panel #4

When a child Tonya would sit atop Ole Doc at her Grandfather Holmes farm and it left lasting impression on the artist. At eleven years of age the first art competition she entered was of stampeding horses. Tonya took the Blue Ribbon in an Open Class Category at Tucumcari, New Mexico's Quay County Fair.
Original of note card art.

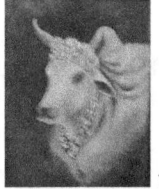 price: $350.00 (framed 20hx16w)
Book Cover: *Sacred Cows in Science: No Objectivity Allowed* panel #4 by E Norbert Smith, Ph.D.

This cover art was commissioned specifically for Dr. E. Norbert Smith of Weatherford, Oklahoma for the book he wrote in and edited for sixteen other authors on science untruths taken as fact and taught in our public schools. All the authors writing in this book are educated in the fields of debate. The book, *Sacred Cows,* is on Amazon.

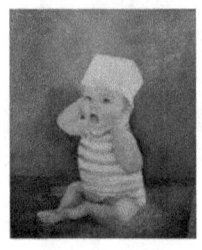 price: $350.00 (framed 23hx18w)

New Toy: panel #4

The most expensive toys are sometimes cast aside for a box to play in, a wooden spoon to bang with or a plastic storage container to wear as a hat. Imagination kicks in with the plain and the simple evoking a new song and utterances.

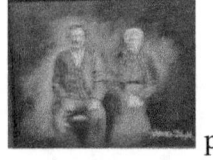 price: $30.00   (framed 16hx18w)

Robert Hatton and Cuma King: panel #4

The artist's great grandfather and her great, great grandmother done in a folksy sepia-tone but still very much resemble the subjects.

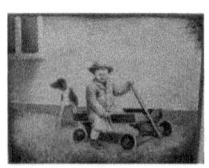 price: $895.00 (framed 23hx27w)

Daydreaming: panel #4

Playtime has a unique history by being in *The Best of Texas* catalog which was sent to every major architect across America. Thirty artists from varying mediums, who were very well known in their craft, and then some were beginners, were in this catalog. After viewing Tonya's first solo showing at the Woman's Forum in Wichita Falls in 1981 the agent selected this new artist to be among the Texas greats.

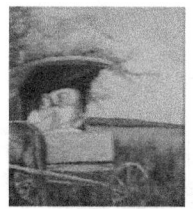 price: $35.00   (framed 16hx13w)

Courting: panel #4

No cars then, only buggies were available for courting.

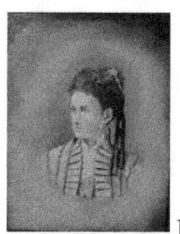 price: $250.00 (framed 32hx 26w)

Unknown Lady: panel board #4

Details of tailoring fascinated Tonya to record this unknown lady's clothing and her coifed tresses with fancy hair pins.

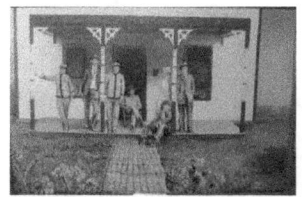 price: $995.00   (framed 25hx37w)

Mrs. Worthington's Boarding House: panel #5

Oklahoma Land Grant Kids going to school in Stillwater, at Oklahoma A & M, now called Oklahoma State University. The school itself was a three story brownstone house but no dorms were available for students. They stayed in boarding houses. The artist's family owned a small picture of a boarding house with information written on the back. When that old brownstone building was restored by the OK Historical Soc. Tonya was asked to have her solo art showing titled, Homesteaders there. She gave the photo to them to have it displayed there. The person on the right is Elmer Fredrick Dowell, grandfather of the artist. His neighbor and friend on the porch too is named Keating and believed to be a relative of the former Govenor of OK. Zinnias was an addition since it was Tonya's grandmother's favorite flower she planed along the outter edges of her garden.

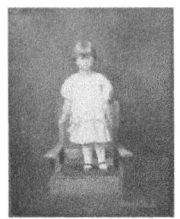
price: $190.00 (framed 16hx14w)

Dotty: panel #5

Born with a beauty equaled with a stubborn streak peaked artistic appitites to preserve this little tyke, Dorothy Rose Dowell, for history.

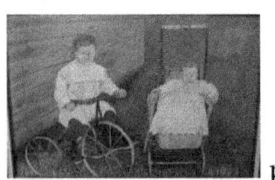
price: $1,600.00 (framed 31hhx44w)

Playtime: panel #5

Taken from an abandoned album of photographs belonging to the late Myrtle Groves of Wichita Falls, Texas. When Clarence's daughter and family rented the home albums were found that no one wanted. They were well documented and were interesting to Tonya fitting the nitch of history and lifestyles of the common man of yesteryear. This piece was also selected to be in *The Best of Texas Catalog*.

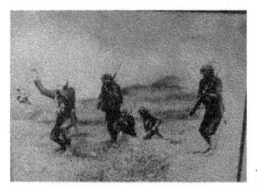 price: $450.00 (framed 24hx30)

Freedom's Price Tag: panel #5

In Perry, Oklahoma a photographer left for the war to document with his camera then came back to set up shop. One day, many years later, someone started throwing glass negatives from a top story window of the now deceased photographer. Some of the glass negatives were rescued and the artist purchased them from this rescuer, her cousin, who had an antique store joining many other businesses around the Perry square.

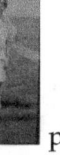 price: $795.00 (framed 39hx32w)

Difference of Opinion: panel #5

During the boomtown days in Burkburnett some photos trickled into albums, one of which the author lucked into. This piece was done in a folksy way but has a realistic topic, a difference of opinion that wasn't listened to or heard until one asserted himself.

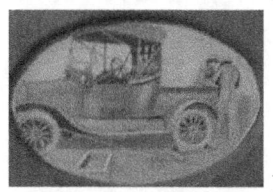 price: $25.00 (framed 7hx9w)

Boomtown Oilies: panel #5

Truck and tools used at the well site.

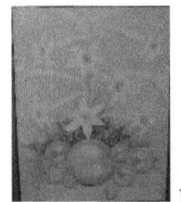 price: $400.00   (framed 34hx27w)

Pearls and Lilies: panel #6

One of the body of works done, *Pearls and Things*, relating texture and pearl luminescence. Many objects were used among those different size pearls but flowers was the choice for these shiney oyster marbles.

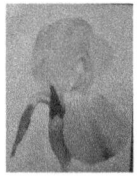 price: $3,500.00 (41hx31w)

Iris : panel #6

The iris was grown by the artist and photographed by Clarence's daughter, Shawn Hardin. This was a period of time when Tonya was heavily involved in painting in a limited palette, one color, for historical depictions. She painted the iris with a full range of colors and showed the delicate petals then takes the viewer inside this marvelous poor man's orchid to show the meticulous color and texture changes. It was primarily painted to prove she could paint in a full palette but simply chose to use the limited one to paint the days of yesterday. Possibly she was saying to her peers, "Leave me to my passion exploring what one color can do," when she painted this iris.

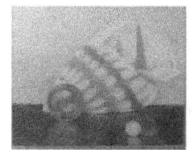 price: $795.00 (framed 33hx38w)

Reflections: panel #6

    Pearls and Things was a fascination for the artist who did a body of works with this title. Textures lured her on to record God's interesting and beautiful creations, even insignificant things if one only took the time to look. Unnoticed things can make reflections.

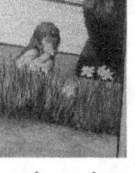 price: $395.00 (framed 25hx22w)

Springtime: panel #6

    Cheryl at Day School while the artist worked. She took advantage of those daffodils trying to sniff out spring.

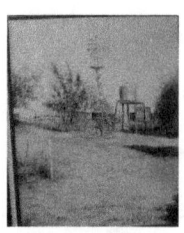 price: $250.00 (framed 37hx31w)

Memories: panel #6

    Hot sandy yards with no grass was the order of the day at this spot known so well to the artist. Many nights during World War II the family sat outside finishing out the day in the cooler air by telling stories of the past, oral history. This is where the artist learned of her Indian grandmother but only enough information to whet her appitite to learn more. Little did she know she would write three books about her in the years to come.

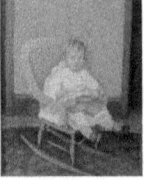 price: $195.00   (framed 29hx24w)

Rocking: panel #6

Children fascinate the artist and this little one with the bunny in a rocking chair also called for a canvas and paint brush. Such a concept leads one to remember the days long ago or for those too young to know, look and listen visually to days gone by.

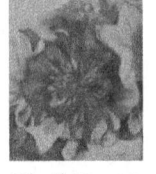 price: $750.00   (framed 28hx24w)

Red Potted Plant: panel #7

Love of flowers and the textures versus shadow play in a real close-up view is one of Tonya's favorite subject matters. The changes of red with shadows emerging from darkest intensities to lighter colors help format her textures. This type interest is done in many of her depictions of flowers whether exercised in oil or colored pencil, her latest medium of interest.

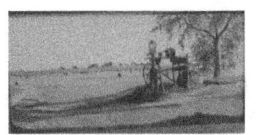 price: $450.00   (framed 13hx25w)

Homestead History: panel #7

The past and the present is conveyed in this oil painting of Tonya's beloved grandparent's farm she spent her summers on. Modern round bales of hay lay in the pasture next to the lane going to the mailbox, all done in a full palette. Relics of the past used to gas up farm equipment welcome travelers into the open outer yard leading to the house are in sepia tone oils.

price: $1,100.00   (framed 31hx37w)

Paducah Family Restaurant: panel #7

A traveling minstrel show family worked in the states of LA, OK, TX and NM. It was time to stop the show for a while so the kids could get an education. They bought a restaurant on this one occasion at Paducah, Texas. The little boy sitting on the porch with his dog, U-know, was a personal friend of the artist, Pop Morrow from Albuquerque, New Mexico. He loaned her a number of photographs of their early day work as minstrell show people and a body of works was done just on this one topic. Many of the paintings have been sold through the years. This piece was listed in _The Best of Texas Catalog_ containing various mediums of thirty famous and not so famous Texas artists in the early 1980s, one being Amado Pena.

Paducah Family Restaurant has been done in a folksy

manner the artist used to instill an aura of yesterday visually. Interestingly Pop Morrow ran grocery stores over the years. His first grocery store began in Las Vegas, New Mexico with a partner that went to Albuquerque to become an exclusive furrier, when such was not frowned upon. The artist's mother got her mink stole from this business many decades ago.

Pop, at the time when he loaned his photographs, was retired from the grocery store business but was the cook for Wednesday night suppers at First Baptist Church in Albuquerque. The church, like Pop Morrow, is no longer here.

price: $995.00 (framed 34hx28w)

Dust Bowl Days: **Buddy Ryan** panel #7

1934 was the year this little fella's big sister made his clothes. Her little brother was the apple of her eye and went on to become the head coach of the Philidelphia Eagles Football Team. She asked Tonya if she would paint a little tiny picture she had of her brother wearing the clothes she made for him. The plan was he could see it when all the family would be at her house for she and her husband's anniversary bash at Waurika Lake in Oklahoma. Buddy and his wife had a new home in Kentucky and might could use some art. Buddy must have felt set up because he refused to even look at it. The artist learned a valuable lesson from this.

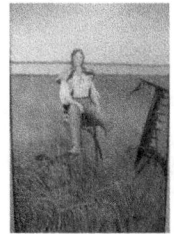 price: $375.00   (framed 43hx31w)

Past and Present: panel #7

Another example of art presenting the past and the present from a limited palette to full. *(Some Days Are Diamonds* is another one) Cheryl, the artist's daughter sits for this one on Jay Shook's old machinery in a field grown over with grass. Location is off City View Lane in Wichita Falls, Texas.

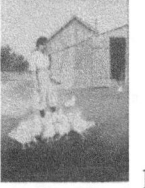 price: $450.00   (framed 21hx18w)

Sweet Country Rose: panel #7

During dust bowl days it was difficult to hang on. Elmer wanted to give up and move but Rose said, "Let's try it one more year, Elmer." Her egg money sustained them in bare essentials. Rose was the little girl from Iowa with a mighty influence in the community, the barber, the shoe cobbler, the do-gooder, always taking up slack when a need occurred. She learned how to do things because her mother died when she was three and she farmed herself out as hired help at ten to learn how to sew, cook and other household chores.
Original of note card art.

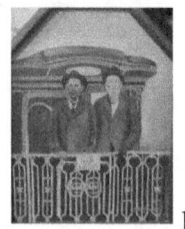 price: $85.00 (framed 16hx12w)

The Katy Flyer: panel #7

This train was the Missouri, Texas, Kansas Railway system. A body of works was painted of the traveling minstrel show family of Pop Morrow of Albuquerque, New Mexico. The place is Dallas, Texas where the first Railway entered this part of the country from the north. It is painted canvas on masonite done in a limited palette (sepia-tona) in an ornimental folksy way.

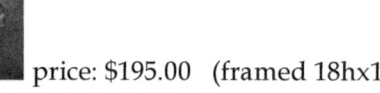 price: $195.00 (framed 18hx14w)

The Tole Painted Chair: panel #8

The Shooks purchased a very old album at an estate auction that had many tin types inside it. This painting was taken from one of those tin types marked, "1865". The chair was a fascination. Plainly one can see it is painted in a folksy way and not realism but it seemed right to paint the past in this manner. The rest of the story is: a robbery occurred from a break-in of the Shook's home and this album full of tin types was stolen.

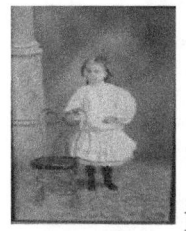 price: $90.00 (framed16hx14w)

New Dress: panel #8

On a very poor dirt farm west of Marlow, Oklahoma, a new dress was far more than a luxury, it was exceptional but this little girl, the artist's aunt, was doted on. Lots of hard labor afforded their daughter her new dress. The year was around 1911.

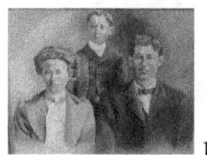 price: $250.00 (framed 19h x23w)

Land Grant Kids: panel #8

The parent's of these three paid the ultimate price to provide a new home in the Cherokee Strip. Six weeks after the farm was staked, their father died of pneumonia after getting caught in an Oklahoma blue norther when going to Mulhall to get supplies. His death left his wife to make this farm a "workinig farm" with her children. She struggled, at times with the neighbor's help, and by the time allotment of seven years their farm had produced enough to make it. It was at that time when their mother died leaving her youngest child, the artist's grandfather, an orphan at ten. The offspring of those who staked their land were called *land grant kids*. Note the tailored look of their clothes. Their mother was an expert tailor and made most of their clothes.

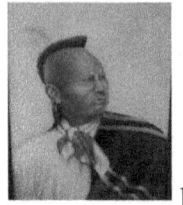 price: $95.00   (framed 23hx18w)

Dog Face: panel #8

The origin of this painting was lost during the artist's move from Oklahoma to Texas. The name of Dog Face remains from memory. It too is from a limited palette but with more colors than the sepia-tone art. The artist experimented with this idea but settled on sepia-tone to paint the past, one color which has varying shades of raw umber.

price: $400.00   (framed 26hx22w)

Eastertime With Grandpa: panel #8

Mary Elizabeth Holmes, sister of the artist, sits between the legs of her beloved grandfather. A paper mache' bunny is at her feet and she wears a dress her mother made for her at Easter time in 1942. The old catalog house was one full of memories, poor compared to many but more than rich to those who were connected to the people living within. Those porch posts were incorporated in the artist's home that her husband built on Waurika Lake in Oklahoma decades after the demise of the old catalog house.

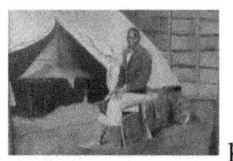 price: $600.00 (framed 19hx26w)

Freedom!: panel #8

Still searching for her lost heritage, Tonya continued the process of painting scenes of the Cival War, which proved to be a stepping stone to the documentary she wrote. This black man was part of the Union Army helping to fight for his freedom from slavery. Taken from a Mathew Brady recording of the Civil War.

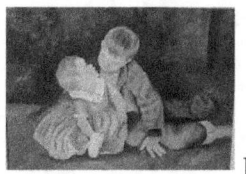 price: $495.00 (framed 24hx32w)

My Children: panel #9

The place was Clayton, New Mexico when the artist took this picture of her children. Her little son was going on six and her daughter was less than a year old. He was dressed in his jeans and boots ready to explore on the mesa outside with his boxer dog, Brandy. Brandy protected him from Rattlesnakes. At this time Tonya was part owner of the oldest department story in New Mexico, Herztiens. This painting was one of the earlier works done by Tonya before she developed her sepia body of works.

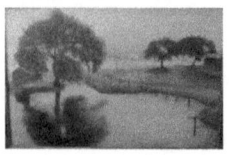 price: $350.00 (framed 31x45)

Perry Pond: panel #9

Long before Tonya grew into painting historical pieces she painted the pond where so many memories were made while sharing playtime with her cousins and her younger sister. It was in this pond that nips at their legs and toes ran them out of it. Later their grandpa made them a raft. Many hours of recreation were had here, lots of fishing after digging for worms. In the distance was the bull pen where kids were chased out of the pasture many times. Homesick for the homesteaded farm, Tonya painted those memories. This is an early day painting as her art form was beginning to develop.

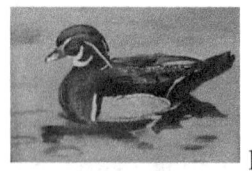 price: $75.00 (framed14hx17w)

Duck Study: panel #9

Reflections in the water, of light, shadow play from the duck, and of course the plumage with all the interesting design and patterns gave a complexity to learn from. This is also an early depiction done by the artist.

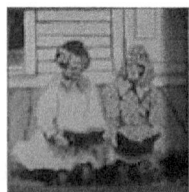 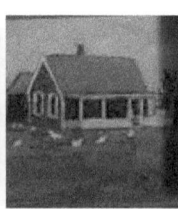 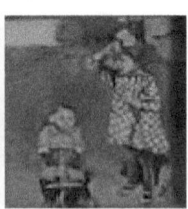 price: $85.00 (ea 4"framed)

Whipple School-Homestead-Claud & Dorothy Dowell: panel #9

These are four inch miniatures of days gone by, an era

gone forever. Even the artist was fortunate to have attended a one room school for a short period of time. That is where some of her mother's friends are, on the porch of this school house in north central Oklahoma. The second miniature is the farm house that grew into the one the artist knew. Some of it looks familiar but it became larger and more modern as the years progressed. And the last miniature is of the artist's mother and little brother around 1919.

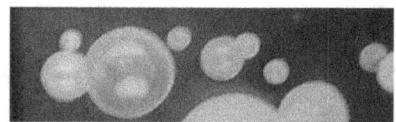

price: $75.00   (9 x 22, canvas on
__Worlds of Pearls:__ panel #9   masonite)

A study of the luminescence of pearls.

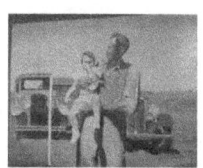

price: $9,000.00 (framed 36hx48w)
__Mixed Heritage__: panel # north wall

"The Homesteader, the Indian and me, bonded by blood, replaced with love where once there was enmity. On this land that we stand free, belonging once to the Cherokee, a purpose was planted that others might see through the Indian and the Homesteader mixed in me." In 1936, the artist, a year old, is in the arms of her grandfather on the homesteaded farm located in the Cherokee Strip. Tonya's background, through her father, brings back full circle Native American lineage into the family which now relates to this land.

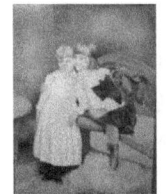 price: $12,000,00 (framed 57hx44w)
Through the Eyes of the Children: panel # north wall
Children used to have been seen mostly but not heard according to past lore. The artist took a fancy to the textures in this piece, the tailored clothes and the pure innocence of children. It is believed that a photo taken in Missouri wound its way to Perry, OK probably during the Land Runs in the Cherokee Strip. Since Tonya's relatives came from Missouri too she believed these children were also a part of that pioneering influx.

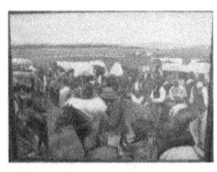 price: $13,000.00 (framed 4hx56w)
Beef Time: panel # north wall
Beef was being distributed to the Indians at Fort Sill because all the buffalo had been killed out. Dale Terry, friend of the author's husband, owned the glass negative of this piece and many others taken by a free spirited photographer from Henrietta, TX, Alice Snearly. She traveled in a covered wagon with her brother-in-law and sister, Lon and Gertrude Kelly, to Fort Sill to take pictures of the Indians.

After Tonya painted a body of works from these photographs Dale sold the glass negatives to Larry McMurtry who in turn gave them to the University of Texas. The university's press published a book, *Comanches of the New West 1895 – 1908*, which has photographs of pieces Tonya personally researched information from Alice Snearly's relative, the late Billie Avis of Henrietta, Texas. *Beef Time* is one of those.

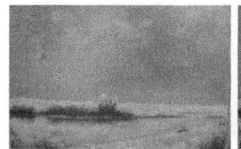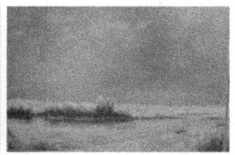 price: $1,600.00 (framed 24hx6'h)

Storm is Coming: panel # north wall

Looking out an upstairs window one day when a storm was brewing Tonya saw the sky congested with white pelicans flying at their Waurika Lake home. This breath taking sight was quickly jotted down and transferred onto double canvases to help give the enormity of action justice.

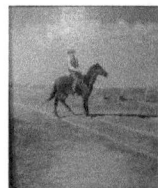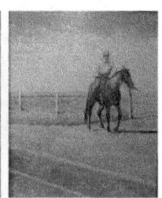 price: $1,200.00   (framed 31hx50w)

Days of 3-S'es (sand, sun & sobs) panel # north wall

Walt King, son of the murdered sherrif of Jacksboro, Texas years prior, was training his horse at Las Vegas, New Mexico where he lived when his mother went through the TB sanitarium. She was cured and they returned to Jacksboro. Their ranch was west of town where the ranch house still stands. The family grave site is on the ranch. Sheriff William King and his wife Cuma Ethridge King are the artist's great-great grandparents.

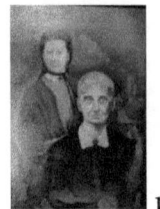 price: $1,400.00   (framed 44hx32w)

My Eyes Have See, My Feet Have Trod: panel # north wall

Sepia-tone oils were used for historical pieces and this one is of the artist's great, great grandmother. She had always heard about an Indian grandmother who was half Cherokee. It took her forty years researching and painting touch stones to be able to put together some history of her. Pictured here is a portrait of her as a young woman and that of an old woman before she dies not long after the photo. The Trail of Tears is depicted in the background when one forth of the Cherokee Nation died during the Indian removal. Her painting hung at the Cherokee Museum in Tahlequah, OK. Three books have been written about this grandmother by the author, a documentary, a novel and it's sequel.

price: $ 2400.00   (framed 44hx32w)

Displaced Cherokee: panel #north wall

One of the characters in Tonya's three books she wrote is Haden Holmes, her great grandfather. Here he is in Oklahoma or Texas, the artist isn't sure. He indeed was a displaced Cherokee but pride kept him from enrolling on the rolls the white man set up to control the population of Native Americans who were removed to Oklahoma. This painting was used for the cover of Tonya's documentary, _Displaced_

Cherokee: Come Home, Come Home, which took first place in an Open Class Category at the 1986 Oklahoma State Fair then was endorsed by the Oklahoma Department of Libraries. All the film used to publish this book were destroyed by the printer. A copy from an origenial book is available from a publisher who records family geneologies.

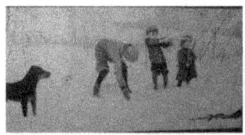 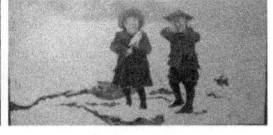 price: $3,000.00

__The Bear Hunters:__ panel #north wall   (framed 25hx98w)

    Two photographs were incorporated to form this eight foot long piece by fudging a bit with the connection qualities for the scenes. Bears of course sleep during winter but a child's imagination soars refuting fact at times. This concept was used giving mirth to the viewer of activity taking place here. Attention focused by those on the right, there was no idea what was transpirinig in the painting on the left. The only one fully cognizant is the dog. He is watching to see what action will come from these little humans.

Cover Art: courtesy of Jay and Cindy Posey of Wayne, OK.
(Favorite pair of shoes of Jay Shook, Clarence Shook's dad.)

www.ingramcontent.com/pod-product-compliance
Lightning Source LLC
Chambersburg PA
CBHW051301170526
45165CB00004B/1809

* 9 7 8 1 5 0 0 9 1 6 1 9 0 *